Now that I'm Older

J.C Johnston

BookLeaf
Publishing

Presentation by *BookLeaf Publishing*

Web: www.bookleafpub.com

E-mail: info@bookleafpub.com

ISBN: 9789357696661

First edition 2022

DEDICATION

To my Grandmother Trudy, for always being my guiding light and source of encouragement.

ACKNOWLEDGEMENT

I'd like to thank BookLeaf Publishing for making my goals a reality and challenging me to do something I never have before.

PREFACE

Nothing prepares you for life-changing moments. That's why they're called such; they forcefully alter the course of your life forever. But although you cannot prepare for them, how you cope can drastically affect their outcome. Writing was both an escape and a form of therapy for me while I experienced multiple moments of change throughout my life. It carried me through the tumultuous waves of hurt, guilt, and shame and allowed me to sail on toward clearer skies of acceptance and recovery. These poems are my time capsules; they transport the reader to the worst and best of my voyage in life. I've learned and healed a lot through them, and I hope they offer their readers a sense of comfort in knowing they are not alone. Life-changing moments affect all of us, and in witnessing mine, may you find some solace.

Listening < Hearing

Listening is simple.
Most people can use their ears.
The sounds go in, it takes no effort at all.
Simple.
Yet, to hear, is difficult.
To hear someone, requires effort.
It takes patience, conscious thought, and devotion.
To be heard by others is not as easy as we think.
Many listen, and claim to hear, but they do not.
They only listen.
Listening is easy.
Hearing, is not.
How can one trust, believe, be assured,
If they have never been heard?

First of many

2

Heart and mind spinning,
Alone, a child weeps.
Cold, dirty, bathroom floor,
Anxiety never sleeps.

Hypoglycemia

If love is sweetness,
Lifeblood needed to live,
I'll die very soon.

Claus(et)trophile

Nothing can match,
The utter comfort,
The absolute warmth,
And sheer solace,
Of a quiet place.

One may find pure relief,
A lack of criticism,
And peaceful ease,
In the cozy embrace,
Of a confining space.

A lack of sound,
The darkness blinds,
All senses are soothed,
Worries left behind,
In the comfort space.

No yelling,
No smashing,
No throwing, screaming, or bashing,
Nothing exists,
In the confining space.

Like a warm hug,
I am safe,
Protected,
And alone,
In the confines of my closet.

Chemical Assistance

A wordless cry strikes the air. A girl wails, wishing for someone to help her. In the darkness of a chilled winter night, frail hands grasp a flimsy paper bag. Heavy thumps of frantic footsteps echo like a drum. The vacant parking lot devoid of all living things, yet she feels watched, trapped, and scared. Rushing to the old beaten-up vehicle, she desperately fumbles with a ring of keys. Under the white moon light, they glimmer and glow like jewels. Their melodious chime as they clink together sounds off in the icy night. Yet, there is no time to pause and enjoy the beauty of the moment; she focuses only on one thing. The contents of the delicate bag hold her recovery. They will help her.

Nearly ripping the worn door off its hinges, she launces herself inside. Blue paint and rust scatter to the ground with the slam of the door. Inside, heavy breaths cause fog to form on the frozen windows. Little lines run up the glass forming snowflake-like patterns. Crinkling and crackling tcar through the rhythm of breaths as the paper bag is discarded. Feeble fingers struggle with its contents; they tremble with both effort and fear as they claw at the plastic container. Inside lies her salvation. Her saviour in the form of chemicals and powder. In frustration, she yells, her scream pierces the silence like a knife.

Violent and angry it is, something no one would
expect.

Little white pills scatter and tumble. Huffs and curses
litter the air just as the tablets litter the floor.
Quivering hands reach down and pluck one up,
hesitantly placing it where it is meant to be. She sips
her day-old coffee and washes it down. The bitter
cold liquid does nothing to hide the vile flavour left
in her mouth. Yet, the relief is nearly instantaneous.
Sweet relief, it is. She leans back, the chair creaks
and squeaks with her weight. Waiting for its effects to
kick in, she grins. It is a first step in the right
direction. She's helped herself.

Death by A Thousand Cuts

7

Heartbreak.
It is something we all feel at some point in our lives.
Some one leaves us, we lose a loved one, we end a
relationship.
There are so many reasons for a broken heart.
But why is it,
That the pain of heartbreak,
Is the most devasting,
When someone gives up on you.

Bus Ride Realizations

On a day like any other,
With the light of youth fresh in my eyes,
I ride the bus with my brother.
At ripe young ages of ten and eight,
We've not seen much,
Not violence, not hate.
Yet as we go,
To sit with our friends,
We are stopped, halted, our path ends.
The burly voice of a large man booms,
And as he speaks with authority,
In my chest, anxiety blooms.
Do you not know of my rules?
To not follow them so blatantly,
You lot are fools.
Children with skin an unfavorable hue,
Hair so odd, legs so long,
An eye I must keep on you.
For whom might know,
What trouble you'll cause,
Should I let you go.
Children with eyes so dark,
Noses so wide and lips so big,
Should not be allowed to embark.
And so there we stood,
Anxiety turned fear,
I thought I'd misunderstood.
Fear to embarrassment,

We began to weep,
At our harassment.
Sat in shame,
Feeling too scared to speak,
Victims of hate, we became.
The light in my eyes now dim,
I hold in sniffles,
To comfort him.
Two children,
Of ages ten and eight,
Have now see much,
Of violence, and hate.

Tainted

After drinking love from a poisoned cup,
Tasting it from an outstretched hand,
Seems perilous.

Yellow-Jackets

"Here's your new vest; you will be the head of our
new campaign!"
I am just a child,
Weak and small,
I do not want this,
Not at all.
"Fear not, for fame, you shall gain!"
I do not want power,
Not fame, not acclaim.
I am hurt, scared, terrified!
They all know my name.
"Carry power over their heads, you will. Show them
who is boss!"
How can I?
When faced with their sneers covered in cherry
lip-gloss.
They point, yell, curse,
They laugh all the way.
They hit, slap, trample…
I want to go away.

Recurring Storm

The storm no longer in the distance,
It has arrived.
If I am there tomorrow,
You'll know I survived.

It's fierce and powerful,
The storm carries on,
It brings destruction and loss,
I'm sure I'll be gone.

Rough waters crash at my feet,
It's filling, I'm wading,
The waves carry debris,
The light, its fading.

The storm picks up,
Frigid waters crash into me,
Like a doll I tumble,
A cry escapes, I plea.

Consumed by darkness,
The minutes, I'm counting.
The water has filled,
I'm adrift, I'm drowning.

I toss, I turn,
I spiral and flail.
I paddle to survive,
Yet, to no avail.

The storm peaks,
The terror, it owns me.
Will I be lost forever,
Out here at sea?

But in the distance,
A light, I spot.
My efforts thus far,
Won't be for naught.

With renewed desperation,
I fight for my life.
I will not be controlled,
By this recurring strife.

The storm breaks,
And through the clouds I see,
My salvation, my calm,
I cry out in glee.

My saviour I find,
In the form of a pen.
Its power saves me,
I will survive, then.

Why?

They're numb, hanging limp beneath me.
The smell of stale air and bleach fill the room.
Blinding white lights above,
Dusty tile below.
A clock ticks,
A drip, drops.
Time is still,
A breath is held.
The old man enters,
White coat, graying hair.
Wrinkled eyes glance down at a chart,
They dart back up.
In them I see,
Swirling pain and pity.
A tear spills carrying grief,
Loss is never easy.
No thoughts run through my mind,
But a phrase does slip out,
"I don't deserve this.
Let me out."

The Grasshopper

There is something enthralling about the grasshopper. How it moves so assuredly as if its every effort is carefully calculated. With its long spindly legs and leaf-like wings, it easily melds into its natural surroundings as if they are one. Its environment is its protection, its home. I find myself envying the little thing, for its ability to slink away and disappear from sight is one I often find myself wanting.

Envious and greedy a creature I am, nothing like the gentle creature I observe. I watch the object of my desire so carefully; I too begin to vanish into my environment. With clumsy little fingers and movements so inept, I lurch forward and grasp the insect in my fists.

Yet, as if unconcerned for its being, the insignificant entity stands still. I question if it simply knows it would not stand a chance against a large creature like me. But, when I open my palms and gaze into its eyes, I see something. A product of nature simply existing in a realm too big for its size, trying to survive.

As we sit at a standstill, I jump at the feeling of a gentle hand on my shoulder. My gaze lifts to a familiar, and far more welcoming, set of eyes. An old woman looks down at me with a face so full of love and admiration that I'm almost unfamiliar with.

Noticing the grasshopper, she takes a seat beside me and together we share a moment, a space, a breath, as we watch the creature stare back.

Breaking my gaze, I look toward her. My guardian, my friend, she bears so much so that I bear nothing at all. But like I watched the insect, I watch her. Frown lines and scars that are decades old. The deeper I look, the more I feel the emotional burden life has forced on her frail shoulders.

Still, she sits tall and proud. Like the grasshopper, she is unconcerned for her being. Mine, her children's', even her neighbors, are her concern. When challenges appear, she stands still and faces them. She too is product of nature existing in a realm too big for her size. But she is there, trying to survive. Standing before her tormentors to protect us all. When problems go, she too disappears. Slinking away back into her home from whence she came.

There is something enthralling about my grandmother. How she moves so assuredly, how she cares so deeply. With the more she suffers, she melds further into her surroundings. But she always finds us on the outside. Seeks us out and draws us in. Her environment is her protection, and it quickly becomes mine. I envy her, I miss her.

Perhaps one day, I too can become a grasshopper.

The Quiet Land

Beyond the mist,
Far across the threshold of consciousness
Lies a Quiet Land.
A realm of peace and tranquility,
Magnificent creatures of wild creativity,
Call it home.
Nothing bad nor wrong exists here,
Only the good, kind, and silent,
Live within its fragile borders.
Its ruler is strong, brave, and loyal
She returns every day,
To her Quiet Land.
After long periods away on business,
She comes home to safety and peace,
In the realm of her creation.
Here she belongs and can be heard,
And trapped within her sleeping mind,
She is free.

What doesn't end you…

The mountain is tall
Yet before it I'm standing
Stronger than before

Love Starved

19

I always hunger
Food is not my sustenance
Their approval is

Sensorineural

20

The world is both immensely silent
While being excruciatingly loud.
This life of noiseless isolation,
Arrives like a dreaded storm cloud.

Grief

The feeling of a heart breaking comes when you
lose someone you love.
But what do you call the pain one feels when
they lose a part of themselves?
Love may be found again, and the pain of
heartbreak is rarely ever permanent.
But to retrieve the pieces of yourself that have
been lost, stolen, and gone for good?
That kind of pain, it does not ever go away.
It festers and grows, like a vile mold. At its
peak, it explodes, leaving you angry and cold.
Then the pain trickles, it fades, and leaves you
all alone.
And you are forced to live with yourself, ever
aware of the piece missing from your home.

The Visitation

A thief in the night,
It stole sound; a precious love,
Threatening silence.

Crescent Beach

Eyes close.
Wading in clear water, gentle waves lap at my feet.
A caw from a bird sounds above, a low howl
cascades across the hills.
Eyes open.
Tranquil hues of orange and pink caress the sky.
Clouds like strands of silk thread through the rays of
the setting sun.
Deep breath in.
Salty seawater, fresh grass, and the lingering scent of
sea hollies carry in the air.
Long breath out.
A tender breeze brushes my skin, goosebumps trickle
up my arms bringing up giggles from deep in my
soul.
Here, where the river meets the sea, in this peaceful
bay along an isolated stretch of sand, I can finally be.
Worries melt away, and all of life's troubles seem
trivial. Clarity, like never before, fills me.
And that sense of validation, I carry with me to this
day.

Catharsis

To start, to begin,
My voice, seems still.
My words, being spoken,
The thought, makes me ill.

No movement, no flow,
In these thoughts, I see.
Mouth open, mind closed,
No words, come from me.

My mind, so full,
It hurts, to think.
So scared, vulnerable,
Into myself, I shrink.

Heart racing, breath heavy,
My throat, it tightens.
My hands, they clench,
Confession, it frightens.

Eyes shifting, foot tapping,
A clock, it ticks.
She gazes, legs cross,
Her pen, it clicks.

I'm urged, I'm prodded,
Words trickle, they spill.
Closed mind, not thinking,
The space, they fill.

Like water, words flow,
They crash, they drench.
Stressed, worried,
The pillow, I clench.

They roll, they tumble,
The weight, they carry.
This burden, I share,
My words, they bury.

She listens, she nods,
Reassurance, she offers.
I question, is it only,
To fill, her coffers?

I hesitate, I wonder,
Is she someone, to trust?
My thoughts, they're heavy,
Get them out, I must.

As they leave, they float,
Like wisps, like smoke.
Like air, I feel,
For once, I don't choke.

Words fall, I'm freed,
My mind, it empties.
Breath slows, shoulders drop,
I feel, at ease.

To end, to finish,
I do not, want it.
This place, it's safe,
My feelings, they're wanted.

Growing Pains

Now that I am older,
I have the words to say.
With confidence and pride,
I am here to stay.
Once scared and tranquil,
Thoughts controlled me with force.
But now that I am older,
They leave me at the source.
Years of trepidation,
And fear of the unknown.
Now that I am stronger,
I am no longer alone.
With the might of self-assurance,
And knowing who I am,
I can weather any storm,
And break any dam.
Now that I am older,
I have faced much,
But my pain is no longer my tormentor,
It is my crutch.